DECOYS

DECOYS

A CELEBRATION OF
CONTEMPORARY
WILDFOWL CARVING

PHOTOGRAPHS BY ERNIE SPARKS

WITH TEXT BY LAUREL AZIZ

CAMDEN HOUSE

Canadian Cataloguing in Publication Data

Sparks, Ernie
  Decoys : a celebration of contemporary wildfowl carving

Includes index.
ISBN 0-921820-83-6

1. Decoys (Hunting) - North America - Pictorial works.
2. Waterfowl in art - Pictorial works.   3. Wood-carvers -
North America.   I. Aziz, Laurel, 1956 -   .   II. Title.

TT199.75.S73 1994   745.593'6'0222   C94-931196-0

Printed and bound in Canada by
D.W. Friesen & Sons
Altona, Manitoba

Published by Camden House Publishing
(a division of Telemedia Communications Inc.)

Camden House Publishing
7 Queen Victoria Road
Camden East, Ontario K0K 1J0

Camden House Publishing
Box 766
Buffalo, New York 14240-0766

Printed and distributed under exclusive licence from
Telemedia Communications Inc. by
Firefly Books
250 Sparks Avenue
Willowdale, Ontario
Canada M2H 2S4

Firefly Books (U.S.) Inc.
P.O. Box 1338
Ellicott Station
Buffalo, New York 14205

Design by
Linda J. Menyes

For my wife Jackie and my children,
Tanya and John

Contents

Mike Bonner
Wood Duck Hen

Introduction

While humans have been acquainted with decoys for more than 3,000 years, no one could have foreseen where this ancient art would take its practitioners in the final half of the 20th century. And no culture has proved more dedicated to elevating the sophistication of decoy making than that of North America.

The earliest evidence of decoy use dates to Tutankhamen's tomb, where pictograms of tethered live ducks illustrate the Egyptian fashion for luring flocking waterfowl. In the fourth century B.C., Greek hunters pulled carved and painted wooden birds on a rope to lead game, pied-piper-style, into giant nets. Early North American pioneers learned the craft of fooling fowl from indigenous peoples. Their arsenal of rudimentary forms, woven from reeds and bulrushes or moulded from clay and adorned with feathers, gave the wide-eyed and hungry settlers insight into how best to exploit the plentiful waterfowl that filled the New World sky.

The same hunting bonanza that gave birth to decoy making as a popular and regionalized industry would ultimately cause its collapse, however. During the late 19th and early 20th centuries, the advent of sophisticated firearms, the proliferation of rail and steamboat shipping and a blossoming immigrant population dramatically depleted waterfowl numbers. Finally, commercial hunting was banned on both sides of the Canadian/U.S. border in 1917.

When decoy makers turned to the sport-hunting trade for business, they soon found that mass-produced wood—and later plastic—shooting stools made their handcrafted birds obsolete. At that point, artistic carving, beginning with miniatures, became an alternative means of support, and exhibitions offered a venue for carvers to hawk their wares. The first official show for decoy makers was held at Bellport, Long Island, in 1923 by the Howell's Point Anti-Duskers Society. This event precipitated the collecting craze, but not until the International Decoy Makers Contest and Exhibition in 1949 did judges recognize a category of carvings for their decorative, rather than functional, merits.

The news of such an aesthetic shift was happily received by a Crisfield, Maryland, carver named Lemuel Ward, who had been whittling decoys with his brother Stephen since 1918. At the same competition one year earlier, Lem, though he had won several gunning categories, had not been allowed to enter a decorative piece. During downtime in their small-town barbershop, the Ward boys had unknowingly been making history, creating hundreds of birds that would earn them the distinction of being the pioneers of decorative carving.

Dennis Schroeder | 9
American Wigeon Hen

Pat Godin
Mallard Drake

Named in honour of the two carvers, the Ward Foundation was chartered in 1968 as a means of promoting and perpetuating wildfowl art. In 1971, the foundation launched the annual Ward World Championship Wildfowl Carving Competition as a forum for judging contemporary works and for artists to exchange ideas.

It took only a few short years after carvers from across the continent began to meet in this competition for the realism of decorative carvings to reach new heights: Cajun carver Tan Brunet unveiled his wood-burning techniques, ecologist Pat Godin was incorporating a strong behavioural message in his work, and taxidermist Jim Sprankle was synthesizing increasingly life-like qualities, such as feet and legs, into his birds. Descendants of earlier, simpler and often passive floating decoys, the dynamic new decoratives dared to project greater beauty and all manner of attitudes, from vocalization and preening to interaction between mates.

With the utility taken out of carving, decoy making had moved from folk art to fine art. One inherited trait, however, connects the decoys that appear in this collection with the gunning slicks of the past: water. During the decorative life-sized waterfowl competitions, these ornate birds are judged floating in a simulated duck pond.

As many as 1,000 competitors toting more than 2,000 birds—from miniatures and shootin' rigs to life-sized interpretive wildfowl sculpture—flock to the show and compete head-to-head in novice, intermediate, open and world categories. Judged for craftsmanship, artistry, accuracy and the rendering of the essence of the species, carvers at the highest level of artistic skill compete in the open category. The world label is held in reserve for a few upper-echelon events, in which artists receive purchase awards in exchange for their winning work joining the permanent collection of the Ward Museum of Wildfowl Art in Salisbury, Maryland.

World-competition rules dictate that a carving must be made of wood, and most carvers favour tupelo, a tight-grained swamp wood that grows in Louisiana. Other materials—if handcrafted—may be used for strength, and glass eyes are permitted.

Most carvers begin their projects with field studies, and many have an aviary. Using photographs, videos or sketches, carvers select a pose for their decoys, and some still mount stuffed birds in the posture they wish to create. Many rough out the pose in clay, a speedy process that captures the authentic mood of the bird. Phil Selzer and Pat Godin, for example, both favour this highly creative and spontaneous step, which stands in

fer to sculpt the carving gradually by knife.

After the bird is shaped, the feather groupings are cut away, and patterns may be drawn individually, to be refined and etched with knives, fine grinders that resemble dental burs, power cutters and wood-burning pens. Prior to being painted, the carving is made watertight and weighted to sit properly when floating.

Carvers are divided about the benefits of acrylic versus oil paints. Pat Godin, Glenn McMurdo, Kent Duff and Victor Paroyan, to name a few, all use acrylics, citing the ease of application and the short drying time. Duff explains: "I like the effects that I can get with acrylics. Translucence is a bit easier. And if you really want to work on something, you don't have to wait a day or two to get back to it." In the other camp, the Brunets, Dennis Schroeder, Rick Johannsen, Dick Rhode and Skip Edwards all use oils. Artists' oil paints are unparalleled, says Tan Brunet, for creating softness and warmth in the plumage.

The painstaking painting stage demands patience and discipline. Decorative carvings are painted six or seven times, and carvers require weeks to complete the process. Feather vermiculations, for example, are applied one spot at a time and gradually built up layer upon layer. The temptation to do too much is a risk, says Duff: "You

sharp relief to the precision of carving.

Some carvers create a pattern for their birds using size measurements, which are transferred onto paper and then onto the carving block before it is roughed out on a band saw. Power-driven grinding rasps are used for quickly shaping the bird and removing rough outer edges. Jett Brunet, who comes from a region where carving is as much social as it is vocational, expresses a popular sentiment: "You end up out in the back all by yourself wearing a mask and goggles and making dust. No one wants to be near you." The Brunets, consequently, pre-

Bob Hand Jr.
Pied-Billed Grebe, Clay Model

Dick Bonner | 13
Pintail Drake, Rough-Cut

14 | Jim Sprankle
Canvasback Hen, Textured

can overdo it, and once you do, it is hard to get back."

Depending on the level of difficulty and the method, a decorative project can take two to six months, from beginning to end. Elite carvers sell single birds for as much as $20,000, but these figures are rare; the artists involved can produce only two such pieces of labour-intensive work each year.

The carvers featured in this book, representing some of the best of this generation of decoy makers, meet three or four times a year at major competitions across North America. Despite their healthy competitiveness and geographical isolation, they maintain a strong feeling of community with shared sensibilities and are the most personable parade of characters one could ever hope to meet. That the tradition has a family orientation—consider the Lucios, the Brunets, the Bonners or lifetime friends Rick Johannsen and Dick Rhode—may explain the aura of goodwill.

Listening to the carvers' tales of 16-hour days and all-night marathons during which they are, by turns, obsessed, frustrated and thrilled with each creation, one understands that this is a labour of love. Most live bucolic lives and are humbled by their subjects. Each speaks eloquently about birds and consistently expresses both wonder and awe for the living species that far outweigh any

ego invested in their individual carvings.

It stands to reason, therefore, that like all wildlife art, the progression of decoy carving must be assessed in a larger context. It is an art form poignantly connected to the late 20th century, when we hear about the growing list of vanishing species on a daily basis. Respectful of the limitations of nature's bounty, these artists lend their energy, many times over, to conservation to help protect the colourful species that enliven our world. And perhaps with their exquisite art, they pay the highest tribute to the intrinsic beauty and worth of waterfowl.

Rich Smoker
Horned Grebe, In Progress

Dick Bonner

For Dick Bonner, a decorative decoy carving is more than just another pretty duck. "There's a constant thing with all wildlife artists," he explains. "We have this struggle between life and art. Carvers want to capture what the duck really looks like but make it look authentic for themselves. Those two never exactly get together."

The carver's most important tool for closing the beauty/truth gap, Bonner believes, is knowledge. His observations of wildfowl behaviour date back to his early days in Grand Rapids, Michigan. As a taxidermist and collector for a local museum, Bonner spent countless hours camouflaged beneath a sheet in the cornfields of the Midwest studying flocks of migrating ducks. "I had a permit to shoot out of season," he says. "When the waterways open up in the early spring, it's a fantastic time to watch ducks. Everything sits together—canvasbacks, teals —you see them all. It's the most beautiful thing, and that's when I began to understand what these birds actually looked like."

Bonner's skill at using that knowledge to render the unique anatomy and character traits which distinguish the different waterfowl species has come to typify his carving style. "Ask any child what colour the head is on a mallard, and he'll say green," says Bonner, who now lives in Metairie, Louisiana. "That's easy to see, but to know what shape the mallard's head is, that takes a lot of work. And what about the rest? How does it turn around differently from a pintail or a green-winged teal? That's what I get excited about putting in my carving."

After 40 years in the carving community, 57-year-old Bonner, who has witnessed almost all the decoy's incarnations, remains steadfast in his commitment to capturing the essential bird: "People often say about my work, 'Oh, another duck with an attitude.' But what I think is special about my birds is that I don't carve what I *want* them to be but what *is*."

18 Dick Bonner
    Mallard Drake

Dick Bonner | 19
American Wigeon Drake

Mike Bonner

During the long Louisiana days when Mike Bonner was a commercial fisherman drifting on the Gulf of Mexico patiently waiting for his big catch, he was also quietly waiting for the chance to follow his big dream. "I had started to carve on the days I didn't go fishing," says Bonner, "but when I was out, all I'd be thinking about was my bird at home. I'd wake up in the morning and pray that the wind was blowing hard so that I could stay inside and carve."

By 1981, Bonner was carving more and fishing less, gradually easing his way into full-time decoy making. Now, at 37, the New Orleans, Louisiana, carver has built a string of successes with luxuriant-looking birds, like his trio of hens—green-winged teal, canvasback and shoveler—each of which earned a first-place standing for its species at world-level competition. (His 1991 shoveler hen went on to claim first in marsh ducks and second best-in-show.)

Bonner grew up in an artistic household. His mother is a painter, and his two brothers and his father Dick all carve. Bonner's father introduced him to carving and is still actively involved in his son's work. "It takes so long to make these birds," says Bonner. "After a couple of months of working on the same thing day after day, you lose perspective. It's nice to have a fresh opinion, especially from someone who is knowledgeable and can tell you whether it's terrible."

Will Bonner, himself the father of three, encourage another generation of carvers? "To carve something like this, you've got to really, really want it," says Bonner in his deep Louisiana drawl. "It takes too much patience. I didn't carve my first bird until I was 25, and if my dad had made me try to carve a duck when I was 20, I might have thought to heck with it." That said, Bonner will let time and patience provide the answer.

Mike Bonner | 21
Blue-Winged Teal Pair

| Mike Bonner
American Wigeon Drake

Mike Bonner | 23
Northern Shoveler Hen

24 | Mike Bonner
Canvasback Drake

Tan Brunet

The carving career of Tan Brunet is the history of decorative carving writ large. The pioneer of a painting style known on the carving circuit as the "Brunet softness" and one of the earliest practitioners of the wood-burning technique which, more than 25 years ago, changed the complexion of decoy making, Brunet is also the patriarch of a modern carving dynasty.

Brunet has been carving since the 1950s, when decoys were traditionally used as lures in hunting. By the mid-1960s, when hunters began to use plastic bobbers instead of the real thing, a time-honoured Cajun tradition —a group of guys sitting around talking, listening to the radio and carving hunting birds—was threatened with obsolescence. "Carving for necessity was over," says 56-year-old Brunet, "so I was thinking about what I could do next."

In Brunet's Louisiana workshop, the tradition was about to undergo a transformation. The former lumberyard owner began to experiment with ways to increase the realism of his carvings. "I had an old gas stove in my shop," remembers Brunet, "and I had three ice picks that I had sharpened to a point. I would set them in the flame until they were hot and would then etch the wood with the tip to get the depth and detail I wanted."

When he casually sent some of his rendered carvings to a local flea market, the response was overwhelming. "People were going crazy over decoys," he recalls. Inspired by the new twist on an original Cajun theme, eager collectors lined up to place orders, and Brunet was an instant success.

A similar commotion occurred when Brunet introduced his artistic style to the carving world. During his prime as a competitor, Brunet took the world championship in floating decorative life-sized waterfowl pairs an unprecedented five times—in 1977, 1978, 1981, 1982 and 1983. To this day, at competitions across North America, Tan Brunet remains, in his words, "the winningest carver alive."

After 43 years of carving, the Galliano decoy maker shows little sign of slowing down. Honoured in 1992 among the eight inaugural inductees into the Easton Waterfowl Festival Hall of Fame, Brunet continues to make award-winning works and to serve as the legendary mentor of his sons Jett and Jude. Together, the Brunet family members carry on the Louisiana carving tradition.

Tan Brunet | 27
Wood Duck Hen

28 | Tan Brunet
Blue-Winged Teal Hen

Tan Brunet | 29
Lesser Scaup Drake

30 | Tan Brunet
Wood Duck Drake

Tan Brunet | 31
Canvasback Hen

Tan Brunet
Ruddy Duck Drake

Tan Brunet | 33
Mallard Drake

Jett Brunet

"I'm never going to make a small, weak-looking duck," says Jett Brunet. "It's going to be the biggest, healthiest, most colourful of its kind."

Celebrating wildfowl in wood has been an integral part of Brunet's family life. At the age of 9, Brunet began to learn the art of decoy making from his father, master carver Tan Brunet. "I was always in the shop with Dad when he was carving decoys," says the son of the Louisiana carving legend. "I spent my time watching him, but I never tried to copy him. I learned what he was doing best." Brunet adapted those Cajun carving secrets to suit his own style, and when he earned his first world floating-waterfowl championship with a pair of ruddy ducks in 1985, he stepped out of his father's shadow.

Today, Brunet's carvings are dynamic, larger-than-life birds that defy the unforgiving wood medium from which they are crafted. Their seamless flow of anatomy, attitude and feather detail is grounded in Brunet's method of sculpting his decoys from a single block of wood. "I carve without inserts," says the Galliano, Louisiana, artist, who uses only hand tools and rudimentary measurements. "To do that, you must have a really clear picture of where you're going before you begin. So I visualize the bird and make sure I know exactly what I am going to do with each part of the body before I start. After I take off what I can with the band saw, I let the rest be creative, working with the knife to get as close as possible to the picture in my head. When it clicks, I know it."

In 1989, things clicked in a big way. Brunet made an unprecedented sweep of the world championship competition, earning first, second and third best-in-show ranking among decorative life-sized floating waterfowl with his gadwall, pintail and redhead.

Ultimately, it is Brunet's impeccable aesthetics and his knack for blending softness and power that give his work an extra touch of realism. "I am trying to make a work of art," says the 31-year-old Brunet. "You can get the bird in any position, but not everything is pleasant to look at. You can open a wing, preen the feathers or turn a head, but you've got to figure out how to do it so that the carving has a nice line and a good feel from every angle. I try to bring out the best that each species has to offer."

Mallard Pair

36 Jett Brunet
Gadwall Drake

Redhead Drake

38 | Jett Brunet
Pintail Drake

Greater Scaup Drake

40 | Jett Brunet
Ruddy Duck Drake

Ruddy Duck Hen

42 | Jett Brunet
Lesser Scaup Pair

Jude Brunet

After completing his degree in commercial art at the Art Institute of Houston, Jude Brunet felt an instinctive pull back home, to Galliano, Louisiana. Rather than pursuing a career in which he would design billboards and advertising graphics, the young graduate envisioned himself carrying on the Brunet tradition of carving decoys.

In the brief four years since the youngest Brunet started to carve, he has done that tradition proud. As an intermediate, Brunet earned best-in-show in 1991 with his red-head drake, and with more than a dozen decorative works to his credit, the 25-year-old carver then claimed the prestigious world championship in floating decorative life-sized waterfowl pairs in 1993 with his ring-necked ducks. Although Brunet prefers simple poses for his waterfowl subjects, his carvings project the same full-bodied look of the birds characteristic of his family's work, with the signature plush plumage that begs to be touched.

While following in the family tradition of decorative life-sized waterfowl, which remains his most popular work, Brunet plans to expand his artistic horizons to include wildlife painting and interpretive wildlife sculpture.

Northern Shoveler Drake

| Jude Brunet
Cackling Canada Goose

Blue-Winged Teal Pair

Jude Brunet
Bufflehead Pair

Redhead Drake

Robert Capriola

Carving is just one aspect of Robert Capriola's inextricable connection with waterfowl. Since the age of 14, Capriola has been a hunter. He carved his first set of gunning birds—six pairs—to use during excursions on the Potomac River when he lived on the East Coast. When Capriola went west in 1980 to pursue a degree in anthropology at Humboldt State University, in Arcata, California, he helped to finance his education by becoming an apprentice to a local decoy maker, Bill Pinches, roughing out his gunning birds on a band saw.

"He saw that I was developing real skill," says Capriola, who credits his mentor with introducing him to both the decorative art form and carving competitions. After completing his anthropology degree, Capriola began to create original decorative works of his own, and today, at 35, he continues to carve one or two pieces a year "to test his patience," as he wryly comments, and to help support his current academic studies.

Enrolled once more at his alma mater, Capriola is seeking his master's degree in natural resources, with a special thesis interest in water quality and in metals accumulation in ducks living near the regional water-purification system. The larger application of Capriola's data will be as an assessment tool for the existing water-treatment system.

Whether through scientific research, wetlands conservation or artistic celebration, Capriola perpetuates his love affair with waterfowl and its never-ending ecological cycle. "I see it almost as a ritual—making the decoys, hunting the ducks and preserving their habitat," says Capriola. "What keeps me connected to the cycle is my participation and the amount of energy that I give to the ducks."

Fulvous Whistling-Duck

Kent Duff

"The key for me is the essence of the bird," says Kent Duff. "That's what I try to put into my carvings." For 13 years now, this philosophy has helped the former industrial arts teacher and custom woodworker to create more than 40 highly successful decorative works. Outstanding among Duff's best-in-show and first-place finishes are his 1988 wood duck pair, which claimed the world championship, and his delicate blue-winged teal drake, one of his more complex carvings, which earned three ribbons at the 1993 Ward World Championship, including recognition as the third best decoy at the show.

When Duff began carving in 1981, he moved directly into decorative works. "I had never hunted in my life when I started," says the 39-year-old carver, who now enjoys periodic excursions into the field. "I came from loving and being fascinated with birds. When I saw carved ones, I just fell in love

with them, and I had to do it." Duff, who lives in Rochester, Minnesota, claims that while he is not gifted in sketching or painting on canvas, his artistry comes alive in three dimensions. "For some reason, it happens pretty naturally," says Duff, who combines his artistic and pedagogical talents to spread the carving message to students of decoy art.

Riding the tumultuous wave of his creative undertakings, Duff persists in his efforts to achieve excellence. "I've never made a bird that I'm happy with when I've finished it," he confesses. "Never even come close. Eventually, I'll look back and say it worked. But that drive to make it better is what I believe keeps me going."

Kent Duff | 53
Wood Duck Pair

54 | Kent Duff
Redhead Drake

Oldsquaw Hen

56 | Kent Duff
Blue-Winged Teal Drake

Kent Duff | 57
Blue-Winged Teal Hen

| Kent Duff
Wood Duck Drake

Skip Edwards

If artistic growth can be compared to the chronology of a human life, Skip Edwards might currently describe himself as a teenager. Although young in his decorative-carving career and already creating award-winning birds, Edwards, by his own admission, is at a frustrating stage in which each hard-won victory pulls up short of his creative expectations.

Edwards' good-natured insight into his technical skills coupled with his workman-like approach may, however, hold the secret to his rapid success. Since he started carving full-time in 1986, the former union carpenter has won best-in-show honours as a novice with a mallard drake in 1989 and first-place ribbons for his 1991 redhead drake and 1993 ring-necked drake at open competition.

The same competitive events that inspired the Lusby, Maryland, carver to turn a 33-year hobby of creating gunning decoys into a career offer him an unlimited opportunity to learn from the work of other artists. "When I come back from the shows, I've picked up a lot, but there are still things I can't get right," says Edwards. "I'm struggling the whole time wondering whether I have the right colour. When you've got a duck and you are looking at it, you think, 'I can't tell one feather from another.' And that's when the crying starts."

The creative process is an individual thing; some artists take it in stride, while others are destined to fight it every step of the way. Although Edwards seems to fall into the latter category, he is still hungry. "I don't think you are ever satisfied," says 49-year-old Edwards. "You know there is always something you've done that you want to do better."

Cackling Canada Goose

62 | Skip Edwards
Redhead Drake

Pat Godin

"People who say it has all been done have closed their minds," says Pat Godin, three-time best-in-world pairs champion whose work is unanimously celebrated for its innovations in technique, composition and materials. "I try to keep my mind open." In his deceptively simple confession, Godin reveals the secret to his influence on the expanding horizon of wildfowl art.

The intimate understanding of nature that is the cornerstone of Godin's carvings can be traced to childhood. "I have been obsessed with birds since I was 14," he says, "and I have a natural feel for them." Godin set the tone for his ambitious style with the help of a library book on decoy making. "The first bird I made," he remembers, "had its head turned around as if it was sleeping or preening. It was a crude carving, but it wasn't a basic-style decoy."

By the time he enrolled as a freshman at the University of Guelph, Godin's childhood obsession had dovetailed with his academic aspirations. He not only earned his bachelor of science degree in wildlife biology in 1976 but also won his first world championship with a pair of goldeneyes. Following the completion of his master's in waterfowl ecology in 1979, the precocious Godin repeated the performance in 1980, this time with a breeding black duck pair.

Godin, who lives in Paris, Ontario, believes that for truly inspired decoy making, technique and creativity must be in balance: "After a certain level, there are no more great technical leaps to make." His 1984 world championship wigeon pair is a prime example of his artistic staying power. "They are quite unique," he explains. "It was the first time anyone had competed with a clear composition of the two birds, with the drake holding on by just a feather." A hidden stainless steel rod running into the body of the hen and through the head of the drake is the engineering miracle Godin employed to create the expressive work.

Unapologetic about his use of nontraditional materials, Godin slivers flexible plastic inserts to create the tousled feather crest on the merganser's head—whatever it takes to give his sculptures the feel he's after. "The fact that we make these carvings from wood is kind of secondary," he observes. "Most people paint the surface, so what is underneath is incidental. Everybody thinks it's wood carving, but it's not really. It's much more sculpture."

Twenty-seven years after he began, Godin is as inspired as ever. More mature in his artistic vision and increasingly demanding of the delicate tension among art, natural science and craft, he remains dedicated to delivering decoy sculpture into the realm of fine art.

Pintail Pair

66 | Pat Godin
American Wigeon Pair

Pat Godin | 67
Black Duck

68 | Pat Godin
Black Duck

Red-Breasted Merganser Drake

70 | Pat Godin
Common Goldeneye Drake

Bob Hand Jr.

Since the day he picked up a carving knife, Bob Hand Jr. has shown his championship stuff. His first decoy, a ruddy duck that he carved at the age of 9, earned a respectable second-place ribbon in the junior class at the 1976 U.S. National Decoy Show. The novice carver, however, was not content with next to best. "I wanted to win," recalls Hand. "So the following year, I made a bird with burned feathers, and I won first place. I was happier, but I wanted to win best-in-show. The year after, I carved another bird and won. Then I was happy."

It was not the first time that the Long Island community of Sag Harbor had witnessed such artistic passion. Hand's father is himself an award-winning wildfowl artist. As his father's apprentice, the young carver honed his skills, experimenting with one or two birds until he started to carve in earnest at the age of 14. "After school, I'd work for three hours. I'd carve on the weekends and during summer vacations as well," he explains. "I learned a lot, but after a while, it just wasn't fun anymore."

When Hand enlisted in the Navy after high school and embarked on a four-year tour of duty in the Pacific, his carving career temporarily ran aground. "I got a lot of wildness out of my system," says the thoughtful artist. "When I came back, I was ready to sit down and carve forever."

And carve he has. Spreading his artistic wings, Hand has since created more than 100 tabletop works—waterfowl, songbirds and birds of prey—many of which have been exhibited in galleries in the northeastern United States or have found their way into private collections. But it is Hand's renderings of the quizzical pied-billed grebe that have garnered the majority of his first-place ribbons. His rare gift for seeing more where others see less has inspired him to elevate this subtly textured subject to the ranks of the "powerbirds"—the large-bodied or flamboyant drakes such as the mallard, merganser and wood duck.

For the soft-spoken Hand, who now makes his home in Jersey City, New Jersey, it is the theatre of world competition that truly ignites his creativity. "The week before a show, I get more work done than during any other week of the year," he says. "That's because, while a customer may not always understand that extra mile you put in— sweating, looking at the bird, redrawing feather patterns over and over and over until you get it right—your peers do. When you hear a best-in-world winner commenting on your bird in a positive way, it's great. And when an ornithologist comes along and says, 'You've really captured the bird,' that's even nicer. I'm not happy with my work unless I can give it that extra spark."

Rick Johannsen

"I've been around ducks all my life, and I like to hunt," says Rick Johannsen. "I hear carvers talking about taking artistic licence and doing this and doing that to catch people's eyes, and I have a hard time with that. Carving isn't about creating illusions and painting detail that isn't on a real bird."

Until 1984, when he made his first life-sized carving, Johannsen had concentrated on miniatures—"6-to-8-inch stuff"—a style inspired by a rudimentary carving given to him when he was 12. Although his carvings became increasingly detailed, the Port Clinton, Ohio, wheat farmer had his eyes opened to the world of realistic decoys when visiting his first decoy show. "I saw people making feathers and painting their birds," he remembers, "and I thought, 'I could do that.' "

Johannsen, whose carving schedule is restricted to the farming off-season, did not waste any time putting himself on the road to world competition. "In 1985, I competed as a novice, and I won a blue ribbon for a canvasback," he recalls. "At that time, naturally, I wasn't as good as I am now, but I could see myself getting there. It was just a matter of time." By 1991, Johannsen had arrived and was the unknown artist behind a best-in-show pintail hen, just one of the marsh-duck hens that most dramatically showcase his carving and painting skills.

As Johannsen continues to evolve as a decoy artist, he also continues to bring his audience closer to his subject. "I like to carve the real bird the way I see it, whether it's swimming in the marsh or whatever," says Johannsen. "Now, maybe that's not being an artist; but to me, that's what carving decoys is all about."

Rick Johannsen | 75
Pintail Hen

Jon Jones

"I carved my first decorative decoy late in the winter of 1977, and I sent it to the Canadian National Decoy Contest," recalls Jon Jones. "I had nothing to do that weekend, so on the spur of the moment, a friend and I decided to go to Toronto to see my first bird in a competition." Upon his arrival, the impetuous 22-year-old novice carver enjoyed an unexpected glimpse into his future. The performance of his lesser scaup drake became of secondary importance as Jones experienced his first taste of carving magic. "I walked into the room," he says, "and all I could see was the best-in-show plaque, a shotgun and Pat Godin's winning goldeneye hen, and I thought, 'Oh, God, it's a real bird.' It was tremendous."

While that split-second lapse in logic speaks of Jones' enthusiastic disposition, it also spoke volumes to him about the artistic possibilities in decorative decoy making. From that moment on, his heart, if not his time, belonged to carving. Jones, who resides in Algonac, Michigan, had first begun to carve because of the influence of a hunting acquaintance. Working as a supervisor for a rural construction company, however, he could only pursue the art form on a casual basis until 1990, when an injury paved the way for him to take up carving full-time.

Jones' jack-of-all-trades' construction background gave him the technical dexterity necessary to sculpt and paint detailed wood carvings, and the same wide-eyed exuberance and spontaneity that first led him to Toronto inform his creativity. "I change my mind constantly," says the 39-year-old carver. "I'm not very systematic. I'll set about gathering references for a bird, but all it takes is one great photograph, and I'll throw everything out the window."

Carving largely by "feel," Jones roughs out his decoy with a band saw, then uses visual references, rather than detailed measurements, to gauge both the anatomical and the artistic progress of the work. "If I get too involved in measurements, then I forget what's in between," he adds. "And if I work on something for too long and really deliberate, I start second-guessing myself and make more mistakes than if I just dive in and get going." Jones has parlayed this gut-response approach into 40 best-in-show ribbons at open competitions across North America and five Canadian championships.

In recalling his award-winning works, nearly all of which now reside with collectors in the United States, Jones emphasizes that carving remains a labour of love. "If I'm really interested in the subject, it's nonstop, and I don't want to do anything else," he says of his 14-hour workdays. "When I see it starting to take shape, it's just so exciting. I wouldn't change a thing."

Ring-Necked Pair

| Jon Jones
Emperor Goose

Jason Lucio

Jason Lucio has been bad only once in his life, so the story goes, and for that rare transgression at 14 years of age, he was placed under house arrest. "I was supposed to be sleeping at a friend's house in a tent," he says, "but I got bored. So I came home at 3 o'clock in the morning. Next thing I knew, I was grounded."

It couldn't have worked out better. Necessity being what it is, the housebound teenager endured the lost weekend by picking up a scrap piece of fencepost and whittling a miniature loon, inspired by a recent painting by his father that showed a pair of the birds. "My father had already bought a book on carving," says Lucio suspiciously. "I think he wanted me to try it."

Inauspicious though Lucio's debut may have been, it was another illustration of the family's deep connection with art. The Lucios' Mount Brydges, Ontario, home is a veritable gallery of works created by family members—Jason's sister Laura also carves, his maternal grandfather paints and sketches in pen and ink, and his father sculpts and paints. "Art has always been in the house," says Lucio, "but I hadn't really done much since I was a kid. Nothing memorable, anyway."

But Lucio did take to carving, like a duck to water. In 1987, at the age of 16, he won the A. Danner Frazer Memorial Youth Award at the Ward World Championship for the outstanding carving by an artist under the age of 18. In 1994, at 24 years of age, he is the youngest master carver on the professional circuit. Although Lucio's love of nature and design also finds expression in the garden—he is a graduate of landscape design, specializing in ornamental horticulture, from Ridgetown College of Agriculture and Technology—the young carver plans to spend his life creating wildfowl art.

While collectors around the world who own Lucio's work—40 full-sized and 10 miniature carvings—can look forward to his long and prolific career, there is one priceless piece that will never see the auction block. With its oversize boyish signature burned into the base, Lucio's weather-beaten loon is part of the permanent art collection featured in the family home. "I nearly sold it once, and then I almost gave it away to an old girlfriend," recalls Lucio with a wide grin. "But my mother now says it's hers, and she will never sell it."

Wood Duck Drake

| Jason Lucio
Ring-Necked Pair

Common Merganser Drake

Laura Lucio

Laura Lucio is one of the few women to gain access to the male bastion of wildfowl carving. At 26, the "duck lady," as she is sometimes called, has achieved her rare status by dedicating herself to carving. "I was interested in art in high school," says Lucio, "and while I was waiting to get a job after graduation, my dad got me started and kind of coaxed me along."

Unlike most carvers, Lucio did not come into decoy carving with a hunting background or with a history of carving gunning birds. Rather, her interest has emerged as the culmination of her life in small-town Ontario and from an upbringing that kept her close to nature. "My parents have 100 acres of wild bush that they bought the year I was born," says Lucio. "I've been walking around on it—birding, watching fall migrations, hiking and camping—ever since."

Lucio's ability to make bold decisions is most strongly felt in her choice to sidestep novice and intermediate competition altogether and enter the open class, which put her up against the seasoned pros. Her ambitious strategy has paid off. To date, Lucio's biggest win was at the 1990 North American Wildfowl Carving Championship, which is held in Livonia, Michigan. There, her pintail hen claimed best of species and best of marsh ducks. At that time, the victory represented the most prestigious honour ever bestowed on a female carver.

Wherever Lucio's courageous course has taken her, it continues to lead back to the supportive and creative environment of her Mount Brydges family. Living at home and sharing studio space with her brother Jason fosters mutual respect and provides the added benefit of a resident critic.

"You get up and carve. And the next day, you get up and carve some more," she says of the months leading up to world competition. "You don't see your friends, and you are cut off from everything. Both Jason and I work in the garage, and we kind of sit back to back. We get excited about each other's work, and there's no squabbling, except about the kind of music we play."

Laura Lucio | 85

Blue-Winged Teal Pair

Glenn McMurdo

The first push that Glenn McMurdo needed to chase his dream career of becoming a wildfowl carver came unexpectedly. After 10 years' employment as a maintenance supervisor at a nuclear fuel plant in Port Hope, Ontario, McMurdo's position was declared redundant in 1989. Although the former plumber and steam fitter had attended only one 20-hour night-school course in decoy carving to while away the winter four years earlier, he had hoped one day to make a living carving. "I was planning to start in the mid-1990s," says McMurdo. "My wife said, 'Why not start now?'"

That second, more gentle push was all he needed. As a hobby carver, McMurdo had entered Ontario regional competitions in Kingsville, London and his hometown of Cobourg. Since stepping into the professional arena, McMurdo has become a prolific artist with more than 90 works to his credit. His songbirds, shorebirds, hunting decoys and life-sized decorative pieces have garnered more than 130 awards at competitions across North America.

Extensive avian field studies during spring and fall migrations, a lifetime of working with his hands and a determination to master complex colorations of iridescent wildfowl plumage all play a role in McMurdo's goal of "capturing a consistent mood from the tip of the bill to the tip of the tail feathers." To date, the most impressive orchestration of the three skills can be seen in McMurdo's black duck, which, after more than 1,000 hours of work in 1990, sold for an unprecedented $10,000 at a Ducks Unlimited Canada fund-raising event.

The creation of such a coveted piece of work is gratifying for any artist, but 44-year-old McMurdo derives even greater satisfaction when he witnesses a spontaneous response to his work. "When people instinctively reach out to stroke one of my birds," he says, "then I know I have created a piece that is captivating."

Glenn McMurdo | 87
Black Duck

88 | Glenn McMurdo
Pintail Drake

Victor Paroyan

There is no air of the tortured artist about Victor Paroyan. Far from it. As Paroyan's irrepressible demeanour suggests—and his record of accomplishments proves—anything is possible. In the eight years since making his first decoy at a workbench in the corner of his parents' garage in 1986, the St. Catharines, Ontario, carver's 16 decorative works have garnered more than 50 awards.

A quick study, Paroyan is boldly inventive in his approach to carving. When he required close-range access to live ducks in order to observe their behaviour, he set up his own pens at a friend's farm. When he needed specimens to understand the minutiae of feather patterns, he assumed the role of taxidermist, remarking incredulously: "Why pay someone $150 to do a mount when you can try to do it yourself?" And when he was unable to stuff the birds on his own— as was the case with the hard-to-find ring-necked ducks slated for the Ward World Championship in 1993—he wangled them from the Royal Ontario Museum, in Toronto, chiding a fellow carver who was in similar straits: "You should have gone there. They've got 100,000 birds!"

Characteristically, Paroyan's first carving was created to fulfill a need. "I had gone hunting with plastic decoys," he remembers, "and I saw a friend's wooden one which was so much better that I decided it would be nice to have my own." In 1987, the year after the creation of that first gunning bird, Paroyan put himself on a five-year course to a world championship with a series of blue-winged teals. The first carving won best-in-show accolades in the novice category at the Canadian National Decoy Contest; two years later, Paroyan took a second-in-show at the Ward World Championship; and in 1991, Paroyan's drake in the calling position claimed the number-one spot for the species in open-level competition. When the blue-winged teal was announced as the compulsory pairs species for 1992, Paroyan hit the ground running.

During the 4½ months that he spent carving his pair, Paroyan was enrolled as a student in dental technology at Toronto's George Brown College. "I was driving back and forth to Toronto," he says. "I'd get up early and drive there for school, then come home, eat and carve. That's it."

In the end, the pragmatic Paroyan took a leave of absence from his studies to complete his carvings, which included the first hen he had ever made. His gamble paid off: At the age of 24, Paroyan took first place in the world floating decorative life-sized waterfowl pairs competition with its $10,000 purse. His fourth-generation blue-winged teal pair earned a permanent home in the Ward Museum of Wildfowl Art.

Victor Paroyan
Blue-Winged Teal Hen

Victor Paroyan | 91
Blue-Winged Teal Pair

| Victor Paroyan

Pintail Hen

94 | Victor Paroyan
Canada Goose

American Wigeon Drake

Dick Rhode

"I always had a deep desire to carve," admits Dick Rhode, but it took a lifelong friendship and his love of the outdoors to make his dream a reality.

Rhode grew up in Port Clinton, Ohio, a stone's throw from Sandusky Bay, a popular staging area for migrating birds and the home of the oldest shooting club in the United States. The region has a rich waterfowl history, which was a mutual interest of Rhode and his childhood friend and fellow carver Rick Johannsen. "We did a lot of hunting and fishing," says Rhode, "and Rick has carved ever since he was a little kid. One day, he brought a block of wood over to my house and said, 'Here. You always wanted to learn how to carve a duck. Start carving.'"

As a result of his natural talent and determination as well as a little encouragement from Johannsen, Rhode has since made a meteoric rise through the ranks of competitive carving. "I don't know whether I should thank him or not," says Rhode, his good-natured joke registering the costs of his own exacting standards. A marine-supply sales manager, Rhode works on his carvings late at night so that he can spend time with his family. In eight years, his 15 decorative carvings have earned first-place and best-in-show honours at the novice, intermediate and professional levels.

Rhode's hunting background continues to resonate through his work. "Carvers are throwing wings up," says the 43-year-old carver. "I could learn to move it around a bit more, but my carving always has a tendency to come back to the basic decoy. I guess that must be my style."

Dennis Schroeder

It took more than 25 years for Dennis Schroeder to get back to his artistic roots, but now that he has, he's making up for lost time. After majoring in fine arts at southern California's Long Beach City College in the early 1960s, Schroeder, who is one of the more prolific professional carvers, took a giant detour through the business world as the manager of a chain of grocery stores.

In 1983, however, Schroeder saw an ad for the California open carving competition in San Diego. "I went down there to see what it was all about," he says. "I was amazed at what these guys were creating out of wood. So I picked up a piece and started." In the decade that followed, Schroeder reorga-

nized his life and priorities and became one of the leading carvers in the field. In 1988, he moved from a suburb in Los Angeles to North Fork, near Yosemite, with a five-year plan to make it as a wildfowl artist. Success quickly followed when Schroeder's ring-necked drake took a first-place ribbon in the intermediate class at the 1989 Ward World Championship.

Dedicating himself to carving full-time, Schroeder went straight to the top. Back-to-back pairs victories in 1990 and 1991, with his shoveler and oldsquaw pairs, are just two of the more than 100 first-place and best-in-show honours that his 80-odd decorative carvings have earned. "I really enjoy the pairs competition," he explains. "Instead of doing a drake one year and a hen a year or two later, you get to think of them interacting and can work with both carvings at one time."

Dennis Schroeder | 99
Pintail Hen

100 | Dennis Schroeder
Redhead Hen

Dennis Schroeder | 101
American Wigeon Hen

102 | Dennis Schroeder
Oldsquaw Pair

Dennis Schroeder | 103
Aleutian Island Canada Goose

104 | Dennis Schroeder
Pintail Drake

Blue-Winged Teal Pair

Marc Schultz

For years, Marc Schultz's father Bill, a world champion decoy maker, urged him to take up carving. "I drew even as a young child," says Schultz, "and it was usually birds and animals. As a parent, I now understand that you have an instinct about your own children's aptitudes." Following his father's advice, Schultz, already established in a career as a heavy-construction ironworker, began making gunning decoys in 1976. Three years later, he was cutting his teeth in competition as a novice decorative carver.

Schultz was totally unprepared for what followed that introductory competition. Swamped with orders, he recalls, "I didn't know how I would complete them all." Taking a year's leave of absence from work in order to finish his commissions, Schultz soon found that he was hard-pressed to meet the continuous demand. Rather than return to his job, he decided to devote himself full-time to carving.

In the intervening years, Schultz, who is now 46, has become known for his highly rendered finishes, a technique that involves preparing the wood surface and mixing paints to suit the detail on the bird's plumage as a means of "capturing the essential qualities of a given area, whether it is translucent, soft or delicate." Although he doesn't regard himself as a competitor, Schultz continues to win recognition at shows. In 1986, he won the best-in-world pairs title with cinnamon teals and has another 45 best-in-show honours to his credit. At the 1992 world competition, his wood duck hen earned a first in species, a second in marsh ducks and a second best-in-show.

Schultz, who makes his home in Denmark, Wisconsin, worries that people may become "lost in his finish." While he admits that this might be one of the drawbacks of his ultra-realistic approach, he notes that "while it is compelling to create and study undercuts, it can also be limiting. When I see people looking at my carvings from six inches away, poring over the detail, I want to ask them to stand back. They may forget to look at the whole thing."

Phil Selzer

Phil Selzer got a late start in his career as a wildfowl artist, but his studied approach has served him well. Taking the advice he once offered his former art students, Selzer has immersed himself in wildfowl studies and carving competitions. "I used to tell the kids in my painting class to go to a museum and look at the art," he says. "It's the same thing when I attend a show. It gives me ideas and the desire to strive harder."

Selzer has been carving full-time since 1986; already, at the age of 40, he has completed more than 21 decorative works. In 1993, his canvasback drake earned a first and his ruddy duck drake was awarded a second in individual species competition at the world championship. "I've never taken a class," says Selzer, "which, I think, surprises a lot of people. I started in novice and was in open competition in three years. It's like going from the frying pan into the fire."

A graduate of fine arts from the University of Akron, Selzer, who lives in Medina, Ohio, taught high school art for more than eight years before turning his carving hobby into a career. One of only a few carvers who has formal art training, Selzer finds his background an asset: "I've never had a tough time with colour. I can look at something and know basically how it's going to mix. So the painting is really fun for me. If you have an art background or are artistically inclined, I think the visual concepts come easier too."

Despite the edge he gains as a trained artist, however, Selzer feels more than adequately challenged by the science. "The tough part is anatomy," he explains. "People like Pat Godin and Jett Brunet have the knowledge that I am still trying to get a handle on." Rising to the challenge, Selzer has become a student of duck biology and devotes hours to reading about birds and watching videotapes of those he keeps in his aviary.

The key to Selzer's hard-won success is ultimately found, however, in his exacting standards and his awareness of artistic risk. "It's been a lot of trial and error," he says. "But I've learned that if you are not happy with something, you do it over. You have to be satisfied, because your name is on the bottom of that bird, and you really have to give it the best you can. You don't have a choice."

Rich Smoker

"I knew it was what I wanted to do, but I didn't know how to do it," Rich Smoker remembers thinking after going to his first decorative-decoy exhibition in 1971 at the age of 19. "And I wasn't going to try it until I did. I have an embarrassment problem." Although he was a prolific carver of gunning decoys at the time, the exquisite beauty and detail of the decorative decoys captivated him. By methodically following a self-directed training programme, though, Smoker has managed to overcome his insecurity. He is now a recognized specialist in geese and confidence birds.

Smoker worked for years as a taxidermist, both as an apprentice and in his own business, quietly creating miniature decorative pieces in his spare time to test his carving acumen. His big move, however, came in 1981 when he began to create life-sized decorative works. "With my taxidermy background," he says, "I felt I knew what the birds looked like from the inside out. The hard part was going from the outside in and still trying to get it right."

The carver's most important task, says Smoker, who lives in Crisfield, Maryland, is to determine which characteristics distinguish one bird from another. Fortunately, he adds, birds are as individual as people. "I've got a small aviary," he explains. "There are 30 different birds with 30 different characters. Even though they may exhibit many of the same traits, each one is a little bit different. That's the stuff I look for."

Going beyond mere shape and colour to capture the bird's individual expression is an invaluable technique for Smoker, who has become a specialist in the "big water" birds, such as his favourite subject, the brant goose. At 42, Smoker has completed over 250 decorative carvings—and more than 1,300 carvings when his gunning birds are included in the count. He has exhibited in regional galleries and distributed to collectors in Japan, Saudi Arabia, Europe and North America.

Despite his carving successes, which include more than 40 best-in-shows in competition, Smoker loves his work for its inherent rewards. "If you can't express yourself through the work," he says, "then there isn't much point in doing it."

Jim Sprankle

Jim Sprankle has had the opportunity to live every American boy's dream—twice. Between 1952 and 1962, Sprankle was a professional baseball player, pitching for both the Cincinnati Reds and the Brooklyn Dodgers organizations. After he retired as a sports celebrity, the self-taught taxidermist gradually turned his other childhood hobby into an all-star second career. As a professional carver for the past 18 years, Sprankle has earned more than 22 best-in-show ribbons at major competitions and 72 first-place honours at the Ward World Championship, making him the most decorated carver in world competition.

Sprankle's home is in Chester, Maryland, on picturesque Kent Island, one of Chesapeake Bay's major stopovers for migrating birds. At 60, he has gained an international reputation not only as an artist but also as a carving teacher. The author of numerous books and the creator of instructional videotapes and references on decoys, Sprankle was inducted into the Easton Waterfowl Festival Hall of Fame in 1992 in recognition of his outstanding contribution to decorative waterfowl carving.

114 | Jim Sprankle
Gadwall Drake

American Wigeon Drake

116 | Jim Sprankle
Cinnamon Teal Pair

Species Index